How To Build An Optimized Website for the Local Business

25 Things You Should Know

By Jim Hayne

Table of Contents

About the Author

Jim Hayne is an American business marketing and sales specialist. He lives in La Verne, California which is 40 miles east of Los Angeles.

Jim Has had three main careers in his life. First, he had the opportunity to minister to young people as a youth minister for both Presbyterian and Baptist churches located mostly in Southern California. Jim did this for over eighteen and a half years (you can tell he worked with youth when he emphasises the half year) before making a change to a new career in wealth management. Working as a wealth manager, Jim helped both families and small business investors plan and invest toward their desired goals. After seventeen plus years helping individuals with their money, Jim has helped many companies as a sales and marketing specialist. Jim main focus is to move the needle in a positive direction for any person he works with.

Working in the wealth management arena, Jim was constantly approached by many so-called advertising specialist claiming they were the experts in delivering leads and he would have great success, if only he would invest in their system providing quality leads. One after another of these so called amazing lead systems failed miserably, and often delivered little or no results at all. Realizing that success was really about getting new paying customers and clients through his door, Jim began to grow his business by studying advertising and marketing and creating his own marketing of his design system. Realizing that the old adage of sharpening the saw before cutting a tree really was important.

One thing you learn as a youth minister is that you do not wait for the young people to show up at the church, but you must visit the places the youth are located and build relationships there. When Jim realized the solution to build his business was already answered in what he had been doing for almost two decades that put together a solution that worked.

Today, principals are the same, but methods may be a bit different due to technology. Regular mail and postcards through the post office has been substituted by email. Although mailings may have its usefulness because its stands out since so many do not use this method anymore. Seminars have been replaced with webinars, and door knocking has been replaced with Facebook and other social media platforms. Asking for referrals from friends have even been supplanted by Google, Yelp and Facebook and other online platforms. Why the change? Simple, we can save time and get more feedback by looking at the reviews scores and even dig deeper and read the reviews themselves.

The internet has changed the way we interact with one another and with our shopping. Not all of the change is good, but most would agree it is the preferred method to interact with one another. When we realize that currently Google is the number one source for research on just about anything, we know that Google is not going away anytime soon. Most Americans use Google to find suggestions and recommendations for the services and products they desire. Getting your business to be seen online is paramount to a successful business. It is no different then having a nice looking storefront for new customers to find you on a physical street, as it is to have that same customer locate you online. Having a quality website that is easy to find online is very important, just like having a business show in the Google 3 Pack would be in receiving new leads.

The quality of a businesses online presence can make or break financial success. Having a quality website that does more than hide in the vast information on the internet is paramount to success. Having a website that communicates effectively by first being seen, and second conveying your message in a way that makes your website stand above your competition should be a focus for all businesses. Having a quality website should never be taken lightly and sadly many small to mid sized business have never even created a website, much less upgraded from a slow and ineffectual site.

This is why this book is written, to help share insight and knowledge with small to mid sized businesses on how and why a quality website should be utilized to help increase new paying customers. Jim has been called the Google Ratings Guy because of his knowledge and expertise in helping businesses repair their online reputation and teaching how to get quality reviews in order to stand above your competition. But having great reviews does little if your business is not found with online searches. Having a quality website helps build your online presence and when created properly will deliver new leads through your business door.

Jim has brought professional and qualified website building experts together to create a new company named the $249 Website Company. Jim believes that having a quality website is the foundation of a solid lead generating system to help businesses grow to become successful.

You can call Jim at the $249 Website Company (909) 541-5987.

Why do I need a website?

There are many reasons business owners don't think they need a website. Maybe you're just a very small business, or maybe you think that because you're not selling anything online neither your customers nor your business would benefit from having one. Maybe you simply don't think a website is within your budget. But truthfully, none of these are good reasons for not having a website.

There are so many customers online today that are searching for businesses, regardless of whether they have a physical location or not. And when customers are right in the neighborhood, they'll often search for the closest business that offers the product or service they're out looking for at the time. Without having a website up and running, your business could be missing out on these potential customers.

Not only will a website bring in more customers, but having one lends credibility to your entire business. Consider your website just as important as the front door to your business. Without one, people will wonder why they can't find you, and instead of calling the business directly to find out more information, they will simply move on to a competitor that does have a website that can be easily found.

How much does it cost to get a website?

This answer can vary anywhere from nothing at all to $10,000 or more. It will depend on how much of the work you want to do, are able to do, or are willing to do yourself. You may be able to do it all, or you may wish to get a web designer or developer that can do it all for you. When it comes to creating a website, you have a lot of options.

Using a website builder such as WordPress or Joomla, you could get a website at no cost, but it likely won't be very professional-looking or give you all the options you want. You could even choose to still use WordPress, but upgrade it by using another web host so it will only show your business' name (as opposed to www.wordpress.com/mybusinesssname.com). This option can cost a bit more money, but you can still do it for as little as $10 a month. This is the option many small businesses use.

If you want a website with all the bells and whistles that involve extensive use of coding and really stands out in the ever-growing crowd of websites, you should hire a web designer. These professionals can give you a fully customized site that includes everything you want it to, with little to no effort on your part at all. Web designers are also valuable resources when it comes to the advice they can provide for your website. Hiring a professional doesn't always mean that you have to set aside thousands of dollars; prices can start as low as $50 a month. Just like anything else though, your website will give you as much as your budget can put into it.

What is a domain name, and why do I need one?

Every website starts with a domain name. A domain name is the address you see within the URL field above any website – it tells visitors where they are. Ideally the domain name should be that of your business, a shortened form of it, or a fun interpretation of it. Having a logical domain name such as www.mybusiness.com makes it much easier for users to remember and share with others, which means more visitors and potential customers and leads coming to your site.

Web builder sites and internet service providers often offer a limited amount of web space along with a domain name. This is okay for personal sites, but it doesn't really work for businesses that rely on their website as part of their operation.

What is web hosting?

Web hosting is a service that actually gives your website room on the Internet. Without it, you would simply have a bunch of files sitting on your computer that no one would ever see. Instead, a web host will provide a web server that will hold all of those files and connect them to the Internet. All websites need a web host so they have their own space on the Internet, and there are many options for web hosting.

Business owners of larger companies often choose to be their own web host with their servers sitting in a back room or a tech room. If you are not technically inclined however, this isn't a good option. Web hosting can become very complex as the servers often need maintenance and updating that requires specific knowledge.

With free website builders such as WordPress and Joomla, they'll provide the web hosting space along with the domain name and webpage templates. But this too, is often not a great option for businesses that want to have a credible website. A web designer can provide advice on the best web hosts out there, or you can do a simple search online and research the ones that might be best for your company. Using these services, web hosting can cost anywhere from $5 a month to $500 a month, depending on the type of server you choose, whether you want managed or unmanaged hosting, along with a number of other factors.

Just know that the speed of a web hosting is very important to the success of your website. Google has implemented a speed test to websites in mid 2019, which means if your website is considered slow by Google, they will rank your site lower than your competitors. Many low cost hosting platforms offer their service by offer services that are slower or have less features then others, and it may take a web designer to provide the advice on the best hosting service for your money.

How long does it take to develop and design a new website?

This too will vary depending on the size of your website, the complexity of it (how many different pages, links, etc.) it includes, along with the goals, and specific design of your website. If you're doing it on your own it will also depend on how much time you have to dedicate to it and if you're hiring a web designer it will depend on your own response time and participation during the planning stages.

Small websites can be completed in as little as one to four weeks, while larger sites with a lot on them can take as long as six months or more.

Where do the pictures from my website come from?

Internet users today are heavily media focused, meaning that they much prefer to look at pictures and videos rather than read through paragraphs of text. And your pictures can come from a few different places.

Most businesses choose to use their own pictures including logos, staff pictures to go along with their profiles, pictures of their building or office, and of the products or services they offer, to name just a few. It's important to use quality pictures, as the better the quality, the more professional-looking the website will be.

You don't need to hire a professional photographer, although many businesses do and it's not a bad idea; but do make sure that the pictures are clear, focused and that they are of the highest quality possible. This doesn't mean that all of your photos have to be formal, pictures from staff events or images that show your fun side work just as well, and in some cases even better.

Be aware that if you have high quality pictures, and the picture is using high resolution, this could slow down your website during download from the server. One reason server speed is so important is that Google has instituted a speed test for websites beginning middle of 2019, any websites that are slow will actually be ranked lower. Image quality is very important, but with many things in life, too much of a good thing may not be good in the long run.

You don't even need to take your own pictures if you don't want to. If you're using a web designer, they may bring with them stock photos that they have the copyright to and that they're allowed to use. And if you're not using a web designer (or you are but they don't have the appropriate pictures,) you can use any one of these sites:

- Google Images
- Pixabay

- Freerange Stock
- The Open Photo Project
- Stock.XCHNG
- Imagebase
- Stockvault.net
- Unprofound
- morguefile
- Wikimedia Commons
- Flickr: Creative Commons

Why should I include video on my website?

As stated, Internet users today are media-focused. And while still images and pictures are good, videos are even better. They're so good in fact, that social media sites have realized just how much users are viewing them and have included live video features so users can post a video about exactly what they're doing at that exact moment.

But including video is good for so much more than just social media sites. And your website will reap many more benefits if you use it. Here are just some of the benefits including video can bring:

- Higher ranking in Google. Google knows Internet users better than anyone else, and they know users want video. For this simple fact alone, Google will give a better ranking to websites that have video incorporated into their site. But Google also gives preference to websites that have longer 'dwell times', or the amount of time any given visitor is spending on your site. Dwell time is naturally longer with video than it is with text, so you don't even have to very long videos. In fact short, compelling videos are more appealing to visitors.
- Put a face to the business. Videos build credibility because they place a face next to the business. This makes users feel as though they already know the business a little better than one that simply places a logo and a few paragraphs on a page.
- Give yourself an edge over the competition. While users will gravitate towards video rather than text, only half of businesses are using them on their

website. When you incorporate video into your website, you will automatically give yourself an edge over the competition.

- Appeals to mobile users. Video appeals to all internet users, but this is especially true when it comes to those accessing the internet through their smartphone. It can be frustrating to read tiny text on a small smartphone screen but videos appear larger, taking up the entire screen, and will perform better than a website filled with text – even if that site is customized for mobile.

What kind of videos should I post on my website?

With video being so popular on the web, you would think that any video is a good video. But that's not true. Your videos still need to be relevant to your business, but that doesn't mean they should always be advertising or promoting a product either.

People love stories, so creating a video that tells that story are ideal. This can be how your business got started, what inspired you to help others through your business, or even stories involving customers and/or your staff. Customer testimonials are great for this purpose, as in a customer explaining the problem they were having, and how your company and product solved that problem for them.

Product how-to videos are also great, especially if you have a product that requires a bit of explaining before its use. Maybe it's a piece of furniture the customer needs to assemble on their own – a video is much easier to follow while doing it than a page of written instructions.

FAQs follow this same line of thought. If you're always getting the same question from customers or a customer asks you something and you think 'why didn't I think to include that in the package?' this would probably make a great video.

In the end, it really *doesn't* matter what kind of video you upload to your site, as long as they are useful, interesting, and relevant to your business. Once you start brainstorming, the chances are good that you'll soon have more ideas for videos than you possibly have the time to actually create.

Should I hire a web designer, or use a web builder to create one myself?

There are tons of website builders out there that have allowed millions of people to create a website without the need for coding knowledge or paying hundreds of dollars for software like Photoshop. With many of them, such as Wix, IMCreator and Weebly, you can simply drag and drop your pages, launching your website in an hour or less.

But, there are also millions of web designers out there and more coming every day. Both come with their own pros and cons, so it's important to consider them all carefully before making your choice.

If you need to transfer your files from one platform to another, using a web builder may be difficult. Many of them have their own unique features such as shopping systems and forums, and they won't allow these to be transferred to another web builder or format. These features are native to their system and are one of the things that make them so great. They don't want to lose that to the competition.

If you hire a web designer however, their skills and features they can implement will travel with them, from website to website so even if you do end up needing to change your website's needs in the future, it won't be a problem for your designer.

Web builders can also seem to be much cheaper at first glance. When you're comparing the cost of $100 a year for premium services through a web builder, spending $3,000 in that same year for a web designer just doesn't seem to make much sense. But consider this. That $100 you initially spent on a web builder will only give you basic services (even if it's quoted as being 'premium').

If you want additional features and add-ons, you're going to have to pay for them and they can cost anywhere from $10 - $50 a month. And if you want a website that really stands out, you're definitely going to want several to start with.

If you're using a web designer that costs $3,000 for the first year to get your website up and running (especially if you're starting from scratch), you may still have to pay a small fee for regular hosting month-to-month. You will still be paying an additional cost each month ($84 if the cost of monthly hosting is $7), but you can also ask for any features, add-ons and anything else you'd like. And don't forget, a web designer also brings a world of knowledge you just can't get with any website builder on the market.

So what's the bottom line? If you only have a small website with fairly simple needs, and you don't foresee needing more for several years to come, a website builder might be more practical. But if you're opening an online store, a news website, membership sites, or you'd like to include forums of other features on your site, it makes the most sense to hire a web designer from the very beginning.

What's the difference between a graphic designer, website designer, and developer?

Once you've made the choice to hire a web designer, a quick Google search can quickly leave you confused. Why are you seeing different ads and websites for graphic designers, website designers, and website developers? What's the difference?

Firstly, graphic designers focus on *graphics*, meaning that they deal in images only. This can be great if you need logos, icons, ads, and other images designed, but they won't be able to design your entire website for you. They typically don't have any knowledge of coding (a few do, but it is limited) and they won't be able to provide a full layout. If you need an entire website designed or redesigned, a graphic designer likely isn't the person for the job.

A website designer on the other hand, will have all the knowledge you need in order to get a real, tangible website. They will design the entire layout of the site, and can also create dynamic images and graphics should you need them. Website designers build and design websites and for the most part, they are all a business owner needs.

A web developer on the other hand, is great at coding; they live, breathe and sleep in code. They can create nearly any type of website you could possibly want, but they are not great at designing. Web developers will be able to find and fix bugs that are sometimes inherent with third-party add-ons and features, and they'll be able to code a website from the ground up. When it comes to the layout and actual design of the website however, they won't have as much experience as a web designer.

For most businesses, hiring a great web designer is all they need. But web developers can sometimes fill in the holes of what the designer can't do, and designers have more experience than developers in many areas. For companies that are looking to build their own 'web dream team,' using a web developer *and* a web designer is usually their best bet.

What should I look for when hiring a web designer?

Once you've made the decision to hire a web designer, of course you want to get the best one out there. There are a lot out there (just do a quick Google search to see!) but you can whittle the list down to only the best by asking just a few simple questions.

- How long have you been in business? This isn't to say that web designers new to the field are bad, but using a designer with experience certainly has its benefits. Not only will they have the knowledge to deal with problems, or prevent them from ever popping up in the first place, but they'll also have a larger portfolio for you to peruse to get a feel for their work.
- Do you have a portfolio of working sites I can visit? This one's fairly simple. If they have work you can look at you'll be able to understand better what they can do for you, and this will give you a better idea of whether or not you want to use them.
- Do they have testimonials from past clients? There is no better reassurance that a company is good than by hearing it from real people. You don't have to rely on their website or the testimonials they provide alone. Do a quick Google search for reviews on them and find out what people have to say.
- Do they have samples of how well their past clients have ranked in the search engines? One of the greatest benefits that comes with hiring a web designer is that your website will rank higher in the search engines than if you simply built a website yourself. Just like you want to see examples of

websites they've built, you also want examples of the high-ranking sites they've designed.

Will I be able to make changes to my website?

One of the biggest fears people have with using a web designer is that they'll be giving up complete control of their website to someone else. And they think that if they want to make changes they'll have to go through the web designer, who may or may not make those requested changes in a timely fashion. But this isn't true.

Most website designers will use a content management system (CMS), and if the clients aren't aware of how to use it, the web designer will show them. This allows the business owner to go in and very easily make whatever changes they want.

Do I need to hire a local website designer?

Hiring a web designer isn't like choosing a dry cleaner or deciding what grocery store you like best. They don't have to be close, as everything can usually be done through Internet, email, and even telephone. However, if you are a person who would like to meet your person face to face, a local person would be your preference. Also you can use skype or Zoom to discuss over the internet and see face to face, so it is really up to your preference.

So feel free to choose the best one out there, no matter where they might live. The only caveat with this is that typically you should choose a designer that speaks the same language as you to avoid any miscommunication that could greatly affect your website in the end.

What is the purpose of my website?

Most business owners will reply to this question with 'to promote my business', but that's just not good enough. Put that on your homepage and it will turn people off and likely lose you customers.

You need to think about what the purpose of your website is to those that will be visiting it. Can they buy products from the website, or at least find the necessary information in order to do so? If so, you need to make it easy for them to find. Are you directing customers to your website when they want to find more information? Again then, you need to make it easy for them to find.

While most, if not all, business owners create a website with the intent of increasing their customer base and generating more profit, you need to think about the purpose of your website before any customer ever lands on it. Only then can you really identify its true purpose, and start grabbing all those customers you're ultimately after.

It's worth mentioning that this is a question that ideally should be asked before you ever start working on your site. It will provide the basic design you want, and the type of layout you need.

What are some other websites I like, and why?

Knowing the answer to this question will greatly help you and your web designer. A good analogy for this is when you go in to get a haircut. You may browse through magazines to find styles that you like and then bring them into the hairdresser so that you don't have to *tell* them what you want, you can *show* them. And a picture really can be worth a thousand words.

Being aware of other websites that you like and, maybe even more importantly, being able to pinpoint why you like them so much, will give you a better sense of what you actually prefer, and what you want your website to look like and how you want it to function. The idea here is not to copy someone else's work (which is a big no-no, even in web design) but give you an idea of what you're drawn to. That way you won't create an entire site, or have a designer create one for you, only to find in the end, you really dislike the final product.

What are some bad examples of web design?

Just like you should have an idea of what you like, you should also have some ideas of what you don't like. You can go about this the same way you found the websites you like, but there are also some examples of bad web design that simply should never be used. These include:

- Images that blink, spin or flash
- Blinking or flashing text, especially more than one type on a page
- Black backgrounds in general, whether you're using light or dark text; it's simply too hard to see
- Background images that are far too busy such as tiled, especially when they're used in conjunction with colored text
- Having everything centered down the middle of the page
- Including too many images, especially large images
- Lists of links, as Google will flag this as an SEO scam and penalize the website for it
- Too many headlines

What are some things I should already have before designing a website?

No business owner can sit down to create a website on their own or with a web designer without already having a few things on hand. Already having some tools in your toolbox will make the entire process easier and help it go much faster.

The absolute basics you should come prepared with are your company's logo, images, and preferably some written content. While a web designer may be able to tweak some of these items, especially when it comes to content, to ensure you're getting ranked high in the search engines, they'll mainly rely on what you can bring to the table for most of them.

What specific functions do I want on my site?

Much of the time, business owners haven't given this question a lot of thought, and that's okay. A great web designer will be able to provide ideas on functions that would make the website run better and provide everything you and your customers need.

But sometimes you do know about a few functions you'd like on your site, and simply aren't aware of others. For instance, if you want a website for your restaurant, you may know that you'd like to include a menu on the website, a map of directions to the restaurant, along with contact info. But you could also allow customers to order right from the site for delivery options, or you might want them to be able to book their reservation automatically through the site.

You may not be able to think of everything, and that's okay. Again, a web designer will be able to help with that. But you might want to think of at least a couple of things to give the designer an idea of what you're looking for.

What is a sitemap, and do I need one?

A sitemap is a list of all the pages on your website. This typically starts as a written document that will be used to design the layout of your site, but it should also be included as a webpage on the actual site. And when it is, it should also list the different webpages in a hierarchical fashion.

Sitemaps are important. Not only do they allow the search engine crawlers to find the different webpages on your site, which will improve your ranking within those search engines, but customers will also use it when they're looking for specific information. Without it, they may simply leave the site and go somewhere else.

You should especially consider having a sitemap if your site is very large, you have a lot of archived content pages, the site is new and only has a few external links, or your site is very media-rich.

Do I need to have a privacy policy and/or terms of conditions?

Most business owners won't think about including a privacy policy or terms of condition page; and this could be because they are simply the most boring pages on any given website. And your site may not actually need one. However, it's actually not a bad idea to include one to protect yourself should a user ever have a problem with your site. And if you're going to be collecting personal data from your users, you absolutely need to have one – this is the only time it's actually required.

A good web designer will also be able to help you outline a privacy policy and there are even samples online that you can use. Here is a list of common things your privacy policy should include though, if you choose to have one:

- Privacy statement
- Information about collection and use of user's information
- Log data
- Information about cookies
- Service providers used
- Security provided to users
- Information about links to other sites, especially third-party sites
- Children's privacy, especially if your website caters to those older than 13 or 18
- The chance of changes to the privacy policy being made at any time
- Who the privacy policy was created by

What is a content management system (CMS) and should I use one?

A content management system (CMS) is a publishing tool that operates online and allows anyone to go into the website and make changes (provided that they use the proper username and password). A CMS is operated through a web browser with no special software needed.

If you're using a website builder such as WordPress or Wix, you won't need to concern yourself with a CMS because that's essentially what these builders are and the system is already built right in. If however, you're using a web designer, you definitely want to make sure that you have one, or you may not be able to make changes to your own website. And every website owner should have access to their website.

What's the difference between a custom design and templates?

Templates offer business owners pre-packaged designs for webpages and the layout of the site. Many business owners hear this and wonder why they would want anything else. After all, if someone has already done the hard work, why spend the time and energy on it yourself? But as convenient as they are, there's also a very good reason not to use them.

A custom design on the other hand is just that – it's customized to exactly what you want depending on your own preferences and how you need your website to function. While this may not seem important to you now, it's going to be in the future once your website is up and running.

The biggest problem with templates is that *a lot* of people use them, meaning that your website will end up looking just like everyone else's. With a custom design however, you'll get a website that is fully flexible in its design, function and scalability, and you'll end up with a website that really stands out from the crowd.

When you chose your logo or the design of your storefront, you didn't see what your competitor was doing and do the exact same thing, did you? So why would you do that with your website? You shouldn't.

Why isn't my website showing up higher in Google's rankings?

So your website has been up and running for a couple of months, but you're still finding that it has a rather low ranking within Google and the other search engines. If this is the case, the chances are that you need to employ more search engine optimization (SEO) tactics on your site. A web designer can help you with this, but there are some basic ways you can improve this. These are:

- Title tags that tell the search engines what each webpage is about
- Meta descriptions, which go on to further explain what any one webpage is about
- Dynamic content that is relevant to the user and that includes keywords and keyword phrases
- Internal page links so that one of your webpages links to another
- ALT images tags, since search engines can't read images, this tells them what the image is and how relevant it is to your site

High-quality SEO can take some time to perfect, and there's a lot to know about it. A web designer will be able to tell you everything you need to know and will even do it for you. And if you're going it alone, take some time to really research SEO so you can incorporate it into your site.

How long will it take for my search ranking to improve?

After employing quality SEO tactics, you should see your site's ranking improve within one month, although sometimes it can take several. Also remember that while your page might rank #1 for one keyword, it may still be lagging when it comes to others.

If you're still not seeing the results you'd like after this time, remember that Google is a living thing that is always changing its algorithms so you may need to do some research on the latest Google news and/or ask your web designer.

Some things, such as the age of your website, also can't be helped so it may just take a bit of patience before you start seeing the pages on your website ranking where you want them to.

Can I hire a content writer for my site?

You not only *can*, but you *should*. You may think that you know best what you want to convey to your audience, and that's probably true. But knowing the general concept of what you want to say and writing dynamic content that will get your point across are two different things.

A content writer will have all the experience needed to write content that is relevant and useful to your readers and, if you find the right one, they'll be able to write whatever you need with minimal direction from you. They'll also come with knowledge about keyword research, search engine optimization tactics, editing, publishing and distribution that could take you months to learn on your own. They'll bring all of this to you, with only a minimal cost that could be far less than the time it would take away from your business is you had to research all those things on your own.

Content writers can also take one more menial task away from you so that you can focus on your business. And they can not only write your webpages for you but also your blog posts, newsletters, social media posts, sales copy, advertisements, guest posts and more.

But just like you have to find the right web designer for your needs, you also need to find the right content writer.

This will include a bit of research on your part when comparing the experience and portfolios of different writers, but here are a few websites where you can find them and get you started on the right track:

- Upwork
- Guru
- Textbroker
- Writer Access
- ProBlogger
- All Freelance Writers
- Indeed

Next Steps

We hope these 25 things you should know to build your own website helps you to make a great site for your business.

However, many people realize that the time and effort to build a website would be better spent making money doing the business they love, or spending quality time with their family. If this is you, no problem, we can help!

We would love to help you build an affordable and quality website for you. Simply reach out to Jim at (909) 541-5987 or go to the249websiteco.com to get your website created.

www.ingramcontent.com/pod-product-compliance
Lightning Source LLC
Chambersburg PA
CBHW051405280526
45784CB00007B/3108